D1095706

SLOCUM: POEMS

SLOCUM

TIM REYNOLDS

UNICORN PRESS   19

SANTA BARBARA   67

Some of these poems first appeared in the following magazines: *Arion, The Boston Review, El Corno Emplumado, The East Side Review, Elizabeth, From A Window, the goodly co, The Harvard Advocate, Io, Hika, Poetry, Quixote, Riata, Unicorn Folio.*

Unicorn Press
Studio 126, El Paseo
Santa Barbara, California, U.S.A.

Published in association with Unicorn Book Shop

COMMENDATIO OPUSCULI DE
CULTURA HORTORUM (to Grimold, Abbot of St Gall)

for Paul Blackburn

Most learned Father Grimold,
your servant Strabo sends you his book,
a trivial gift and of no account, only for that,
seated in your own garden, where peach and apple
cast their ragged opacities
and your small students, laughing, gather
the shining or furred fruit and carry it to you
clutched to the stomach with both hands,
or store it away in bushels,
you might find some utility in it — more,
that you may prune it back,
strengthen, fertilize, transplant it
as seems best to you.
       So may you at last
be brought to such flourishing
as grapples God's trellis toward
the evergreening of unwithering life:
this may Father, Son and Früitful Spirit grant you.

(Walafrid Strabo, 809-49)

CONTENTS

THE ADVICE   11

As-tu des yeux pour...   12

SPIEL   13

Blood still tacky on...   14

MAN IN THE MIDDLE OF THE STREET   15

BIOGRAPH   16

CARNAVAL   17

SAGITTARIUS-SONG   22

SHADY LADY, FADING   23

TWO FROM CATULLUS   24

Downhill from the time...   25

CATFISH GOODBYE   26

If you would please take off...   27

SLOCUM   28

KALEIDOSCOPE   29

It's not that I don't trust you I...   35

FOR "PAPA JOHN" JOSEPH ON HIS 90th BIRTHDAY   36

That Hibiscus (KONA...   37

Get in trouble over fifty, he told me,
Hit the gas, man, brakes won't do shit for you.

He had the biggest Harley and blackest jacket
In Oregon, I guess he ought to know.

Not like they teach things at St Vincent's:
Metodo del ritmo solamente.

As-tu des yeux pour
Avril? J'en ai, I said.
Elle a des yeux
pour toi.

And she did. I did. God
made me so laugh
who heard
laughed with me.

(As jukeboxes. Or
10th Avenue, morning, the
birds! Nerve-
song! The city!)

Where there is no
in or out of
season, no, but from below
frostline that hemorrhage,

scoffing
lobster on the
hot rocks at
Gloucester.

Which is *why* you
laugh, it's
spring, love, you have
eyes.

You are revolted by my "external
appearance" (a joke) and by my
stench. Naturally. But you must understand
I am in pain. As you are. Being
this way. Inside
out. These orchid-colored
organs dangling from my
"skin" like a full field pack, messkit,
bayonet, grenades, intrenching
tool, canteen, bandoliers, are subject to
cold. Are unaccustomed
to fluctuations of temperature. You
who believe yourselves solid inside
like a potato, or hollow, lined with
porcelain, love me. It
can happen any time. Fallout,
thalidomide, inspiration, it can happen to you.
Tomorrow. Or yours. *I* love me. Even
so. We love
regardless. It is usually us.

These signed photographs cost only 35¢.

Blood still tacky on
cheekbone and torn
elbow, hair

sparkling with powdered
windshield, Reynolds
is pounding his

Olympia
already — a meditation on
close things.

Asshole! How
would *you* know? Will
nothing teach you, ever?

MAN IN THE MIDDLE OF THE STREET

for Jim Harrison

The day's noise was draining away in my mind
                and the light from behind my eyes
when savage Cypris grabbed a handful of my hair
                and yanked me up
                and gave me hell, so
You, my creature-cocksman, mine, my gashhound,
you *I catch sleeping alone?*
                                Get on with it!
So I leap up and barefoot, bathrobe flapping
I rush down every alley in town
                                and reach the end of none.
Like a man chasing a bus running one minute
                the next embarrassed to run
afraid to go home
                terrified of looking silly
                                standing here like this
                                in the middle of an empty street
                                hearing not one human voice
                                no sound but an occasional backfire
                                                not so much as a dog.
Am I the only man in town without a bed I can go to?
No pension plan
                        hard goddess
                                for your oldest campaigners?

(Petronius)

Dimple
almost eradicated, behind
the ears the
scars, sandy

hair blacked, fingertips
acid-chewed — but
Melvin H
Purvis' fed heart

"pounded as he saw
again the
face" etc (he
had seen him once before en

route from Arizona
to Crown Point.) It
was that mustache: that, only
to whisper in night's

commonness, "Baby, I
can trust
you — I'm John
Dillinger." And

there it was, the
mustache. Love
is not
love, your gold-

rimmed spectacles in-
sufficient disguise. Suspecting
nothing he (no
killer) got it: where

you have that itch

a sequence from Que

> *"Answer as there is to all*
> *unask" & stopped*
> *there. Is it after all you I can't be? Look,*
> *there are letters &*
>
> *poems, & we*
> *aren't letters, Lynne.*
>   *Your*
> *light's off, but look, no, only*
> *Andromeda, blurry*
>
> *thumbprint these*
> *December nights. &*
> *that mother's a right*
> *far piece, & moving out.*
>
> *& not poems*
>   Ann Arbor, 12.66

1

What was I
there, then, or
who, or among whom, or
was I? In that storm of masks &

mariachis & fuegos artificiales, yo
ya no fui yo ni mi casa
tu casa.
        Maricones,
machismo's

flipside, canter, & among these snows
of falling burnings still
always & always
masked a fist-sized moon

2

CAYÓ, over my café
con leche, COMO
METEORO. He'll
rate a crater on the dark side

anyhow. Earle
a pockhole?
No.
                    FALLÓ
EL PARACAIDAS, ours

too somewhere, I fall &
fall, we
fall, Lu-
cretius, where is thy Swerve?

3

This stillness of things
falling. I clasp its knees, its
beard: Do not
kill me. But nothing I can say,

do, drowns that

silence when the V-1
cuts out, that silence of fires
falling the ai-yip-yips &
marimbas counter-

point. It

does not love me, floats
no manly
compassion down, as:
Patroklos, your better, died;

or: me, me, me, me, me

4

Dee Duerson & the
boy in the blue
sweater, Judson, Avril, Ellen
& who else have I

betrayed today?

Mary K,
of course, &
Anthony, & Bob
& Sam & Vivian & Janet &

Bill. Lynne. Hannah. The

usual crowd, no end
to these redheads in turquoise
sweaters   .
                  & I is a
watchbird watching

us: & who have *you* screwed today?

5

¡PAREN! ME GUÍAN
MAL, NO
COMPRENDEN?
           They're sluicing confetti

down the Portal sewers.
My cuffs are full.
         & one enormous
ash drifted, last
night, through my window, from some

fire in the sky.
         Carnaval
itself was tired, you could
feel it. Feel it. Stop it. It's going
wrong, can't you

understand?

6

Done. Booms, radiances
fall, face falls
away, dwindling back black corridors
of hell home, where you learned
survival: when the blind

matador lumbers close, you scream: "I'm Nobody!
Nobody!"
                    Only, viajera tan
perseverante, that
I loved you when I saw you
shipwrecked, eyes
ensimismados, cloudy with other cities &

islands, some
horrible. That, & you were gone again, tacking home

forever.
                    I
cried for you just now, &
for Earle, myself, Komarov, sailor who wore your
simple skin so proudly.
                            Carnaval's

done.
            Nobody home.   Nobody

                            Veracruz, 4.67

SAGITTARIUS-SONG

for William Arrowsmith

Is here no telephone?

Where there was a gas station's your
wall. Well,
that to be said for us, we've
raised our level. Blood

flowers in the works and
bam, that, but too much the bad pin-
ball bings
off three bumpers and

gone, like a dose of salts, thoughts
and all. Still, will you
clear one damn night,
Maecenas, for Mahagonny? Not

tonight. Tonight
the wall, only the wall, lost
desires, etc, pot
calling the coital back. I'll leave this

in your faculty mailbox
tomorrow, Bill. Tonight können
uns und euch und niemand helfen. Tonight
I remember the wall and am the wall.

for Mary K

You walk by Lake Pontchartrain
At this nice time when things grow
Closer (as grass water color
Water colored
Tree trees
Sky) until your sweet head is drained
Of whatever is not the waves' little smackings

And it is the nicest time there when you are
Anonymous through and through
Thinking water colored thoughts if anything
Camouflaged as a leaf
Or a pretty flower
Only a night colored person walking in a night
Simple as sky wave leaf grass limpid as air

(c 58)

Sandy: Anita, our
Anita, Anita I —
we — more than anything we
had or were like to
have, loved —
remember Anita? — 's gulping down strangers' sperm
in Sting Rays parked where only the light doesn't come

(c 52)

So, Reynolds? You won't quit yet?
The goiter Johnson gabbling in Manila, he wants "a
          more preposperous Asia", wants "Peace" —
McNamara, a good family man, fully insured, soybean
     compound "flesh" heated to 98.6 honorary degrees
     over his stainless steel armature, spitshined
                         right down to asshole,
Sucktory of (sic) Defence?
                    And still won't quit?

for Susan

Downhill from the time
bombed house, down by the clear

Acequia in the sweet grass
we lay heaped in cataracting

fire, stinking, gorged
with sun, the abandoned dead

of plague or war.
Flies, gnats, drifted around us

in gemmy clouds, ants
inched us all over,

millions of shimmering
things in the soil ate at us.

Only the alive had found us
distasteful. We steamed like manure.

Come time to live our souls lumbered
back to their hives'

twisted sunlessnesses on straining
wings, honey-sacs flame-

crammed. We went
heavy, secreting the gold they'd brought.

CATFISH GOODBYE

for Marcia

Outrage first when you
find yourself
a fish, it seems
unfair, you miss that
opposable thumb. But come
gradually to find it

simpler so, nudging
carrion at the shifting bottom
where the light
hardly sifts down, grain by
green grain, nosing detritus
for the almost

anything you can make flesh of,
who could not, man,
make yourself meat. Last you
are the river, its
thick movement circles in your sluggish
arteries, bearing you down

to an opening-out you begin
to sense dully, lazing
whiskery deep and green under
flowerpot embankments
silted with our loess, our
seed, our best wishes

So long so long

If you would please take off
the top of my
head you'd
find sand there, and coarse grasses, and

we lay there in the sun,
in the sand, half
buried, glad for the time
being. (At Wingra once

and with my right eye
closed the many children were running
in grass, but when
I closed my left they were

barred in cages,
and running.) That once (I
never told you)
I touched you in rage

but (because I was so deep
in sand there
was nothing to
be done and my mouth was filled with sand

SLOCUM

for Earle

"You man come 'lone?"
Again I answered, "Yes."
"I don't believe that. You had other
mans, and you eat 'em."

The jungle's manic racket (diminished
by distance, screech, yammer and roar
compressed to one blurred sound over
the wind's whine and waves' sloshing,

the rigging's perpetual saddle-creak)
carries to him in an offshore breeze
sometimes. For the rest it's himself he gnaws
the salty heart out of for hardtack,

having "no dorg nor no cat", sailing alone
with a lank crew of slicker-draped broomsticks
on the *Spray,* his homemade world calked
with his flesh and ballasted with his bone.

The water's a rank jungle under him
of soundless ravening; under that green's
a black chockful of strangers' bones.
If your walls crumble, Joshua, can you swim?

Cannibal! Cannibal! I try to understand.
There's bad blood in us. I loved you once,
I love you now. Can you smell land,
out there? Where have they gone, our sons?

a sequence from Que

para Isabel,
que me regala un caleidoscopio

1

"Donde se cruzan dos
calles cuatro
cantinas", where
we passed, '56, strangeness

to me te
tuteando in mud, brick &
rut. To
say what? Te

quiero, Isabel,
whatever
wilderness of mirrors that
puts us in, all what's

real, but changed

2

Time

      taken time
      given, an
      exchange, can-
      tina, Calle

      de Mina: Twist

      y gritos, La ví
      allá, No puedo comprar mi
      amor, Ella te ama, time
                      gone &
changed in that going   .
                       It was all there
    always, with Desmond in the Oxford

Grille ('s always there)
that misery I can't
reach: but
               Driving back from New
Hampshire with liquor I pulled over, to
listen: I want to hold your hand

3

Haunts your closed face some
Toltec father's
deathbound profile, alien
as Teotihuacan's godborn

geometry, core -
cold still in all that spill
of sun, a
waterfall of shining children down the

Pyramid of the Moon, your closed
face, whose
strangeness
bewilders me — open your

eyes, *your* eyes

4

hemos derrocado a un tirano después de años de lucha,
vamos a realizar la más grande revolución de este siglo,
este país será transformado de una manera que usted no imagina,
todo eso hemos hecho y vamos a hacer y usted viene de México
a preguntar cuándo nos quitamos las barbas

El Ché, a un corresponsal, 1. 6. 59

Bearded ghost, everywhere,
nowhere, spirit
over the waters, in the air, on the
streets of Haiphong, La Paz, Detroit (I

felt your passing at

Antioch, San
Francisco, Watts — the man at the corner
with his son, that gesture: remember,
it was *us* did this — & my hair

stood up), ghost haunted by

fusilados, sombra, hombre, somewhere, how, you
share this Orion we're under, help us help it
come, for David, Rolando, Anthony,

Ché, no,

don't shave

5

it's some way of seeing I chase across a time
        of linked spaces
                chased by shining & harrassing eyes
                time is water lapsing through fingers
you are my flesh
        no one else watches me
                with those eyes of a lost owl
                eyes that put names to things &
                        strip names from things
I fall unsouled down some well where colors whirl
                float in a soft shining
your hands hold me up without touching me
things' souls turn toward me
with the key I've taken from the dark casebox of your heart
        I unlock words
        & they drop down over things
        & fold about them
                own as their skins

(after Isabel Fraire, "persigo una mirada" in
Revista de Bellas Artes, mayo/junio '66)

6

Nothing
smaller than a real world
to hold our heads full of worlds —
everything, everything,

young whores in
Osaka chanting after me *Barū
mūn, yu sa mi standīn arón,* beer-
stench & endless rain in

Monterrey, our
loves, our children, our
memories of hell, terror, light, stranger,
light where these dark

lives cross

México DF, 7. 67

It's not that I don't trust you I
don't turn my back to you, ever; it's
this lump, on my right
shoulderblade, low down, of
considerable size. It's been there,
oh, I can't remember how long. I can just
barely see it in mirrors and
can't touch it — or just barely.
I've been informed it's there. And am
ashamed, naturally. But
it's my lump, a distinction I wouldn't
willingly be without —
couldn't and be me.
"An incipient hunch? A
wing sprouting? A new head?"
I think not. In all these years it's hardly
altered. But my body's gone
to hell in other ways as well:
it hardly seems worth my shame
or pride any more, my lump. And yes,
if I loved you,
I would turn my back.

Moonsheeny nacrop-
olis of salt planted
and plowed under
the regular acre

   I got Miss Lulu White Lord on my mind

A white allegorical
Silence broods over us all
a decorous goddess
and our kids sleep cool and nice

   Say I got that Miss Lulu White
                  ooeee on my mind

Where Storyville
gone to seed under ground
that rude
sound still

   Sometimes I wonder where she gone to
              if they doing her all right

i.

That hibiscus (KONA,
DOUBLE PINK, a
yellow slip to say)
you gave us

works:
meaning you
gave it with
feelings hard to speak of, so

spoken of, and we took it, still
nothing to say. But
it's here by our bed
in a clay pot,

both blossoms
going fast now. Meaning
only, we
have it now, by

our bed, will
have it,
pinker yet for the wordlessness of
its going, and have you.

ii.

What we have most's not
earned, 's given us
by some
grace; we

pick it up and read,
remember badly when the book's
away, but it was there
to hand, is to

mind, a way
made to take and
keep what we'd not thought
to ask, hibiscus.

1,000 copies of the second printing of this book were published by Unicorn Press, including 250 cloth-bound.

Typography by Alan Brilliant. Printed by Noel Young